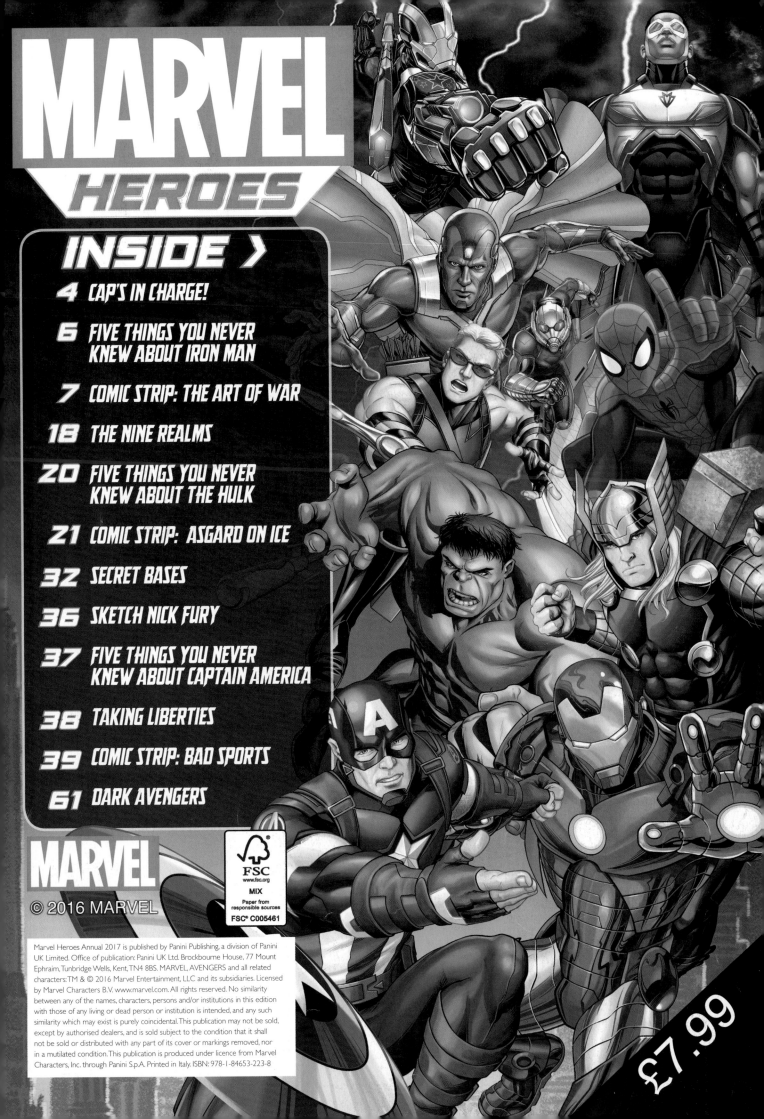

MARVEL
HEROES

INSIDE ›

MARVEL

© 2016 MARVEL

FSC
www.fsc.org
MIX
Paper from responsible sources
FSC® C005461

Marvel Heroes Annual 2017 is published by Panini Publishing, a division of Panini UK Limited. Office of publication: Panini UK Ltd. Brockbourne House, 77 Mount Ephraim, Tunbridge Wells, Kent, TN4 8BS. MARVEL, AVENGERS and all related characters: TM & © 2016 Marvel Entertainment, LLC and its subsidiaries. Licensed by Marvel Characters B.V. www.marvel.com. All rights reserved. No similarity between any of the names, characters, persons and/or institutions in this edition with those of any living or dead person or institution is intended, and any such similarity which may exist is purely coincidental. This publication may not be sold, except by authorised dealers, and is sold subject to the condition that it shall not be sold or distributed with any part of its cover or markings removed, nor in a mutilated condition. This publication is produced under licence from Marvel Characters, Inc. through Panini S.p.A. Printed in Italy. ISBN: 978-1-84653-223-8

£7.99

CAP'S IN CHARGE!

Part of being a good leader is making the right choices for the team. Captain America knows how to do that, but do you? Test your decision-making skills with these training scenarios, then count up your points!

FIRST THINGS FIRST

Do you know your priorities? Out of these three threats, tick the one which you would report as the most urgent!

A FIRE HAZARD

Something's caught fire at Stark Industries! Oh wait, it's just Iron Man burning his toast again...

B HYDRA ATTACK

The helicarrier and all passengers are in extreme danger. Send for back-up immediately!

C IMPOSSIBLE MAN PRANK

Ugh. This bonkers alien has hidden stink bombs all over the tower! Smells like feet!

RIDE IN STYLE

If you and the entire team had to get to a place ASAP, which mode of transport would you choose?

A AVENJET
Maximum speed: 2000 mph
Capacity: 7 seats

B QUINJET
Maximum speed: 1600 mph
Capacity: 7 seats

C SKY-CYCLE
Maximum speed: 380 mph
Capacity: 1 seat

FIGHTING FOES

Could you combat the enemy? Draw a line to pair each Avenger with the villain that they are best suited to battle!

1.

B.

C.

A.

Z.

3.

FIRST THINGS FIRST: If you chose A) 1 points, B) 2 points, C) 0 points. RIDE IN STYLE: A) 2 points, B) 1 points, C) 0 point. FIGHTING FOES: A-2, B-1, C-0. If you got 0 correct =1 point, 1 correct = 2 points, 3 correct = 3 points.

COULD YOU LEAD THE TEAM?

COUNT YOUR POINTS!

0-2 POINTS

Man, your decisions are poor! The team would crumble under your lousy leadership... try again?

3-4 POINTS

Nice! You're awesome... as second in command. Not top position, but hey there's room for improvement!

5-6 POINTS

Now THAT's what I call leadership, soldier! You're made of the right stuff!

5 THINGS YOU NEVER KNEW ABOUT...
IRON MAN

1.

Designed to contend with the world's strongest villains, Tony Stark's Iron Man armour can easily lift 100 tonnes!

2.

Tony once implanted a technology called Extremis into the Iron Man suit, allowing him to store its inner 'skin' in his bones and control all of his powers mentally!

3.

Since the hero built the crude Mk. I version of the suit, he has created an Iron Man for almost every occasion: space flight, a stealth suit – even one for fighting the mighty Thor!

4.

...and it's not just Thor he's battled! Over the years, the Armoured Avenger has had to duke it out with many of his allies: Spider-Man, Captain America, and the incredible Hulk!

5.

When stranded in a faraway fantasy realm, Tony's genius was really put to the test. He transformed the Iron Man suit into a mechanical marvel, and used a sword to fight!

NEW YORK CITY.

IRON MAN, HOW'S IT LOOKING DOWN THERE?

LIKE SOMEONE'S KICKED OVER AN ANT HILL, CAP. PEOPLE ARE SCATTERING IN ALL DIRECTIONS, BUT FROM WHAT, I CAN'T TELL.

THEY JUST STARTED... MOVING!

THEY'RE COMING THIS WAY! THEY'RE ALIVE!

"ALIVE?" WHO'S ALI--?

UHH...CAP? YOU'RE NOT GOING TO BELIEVE THIS.

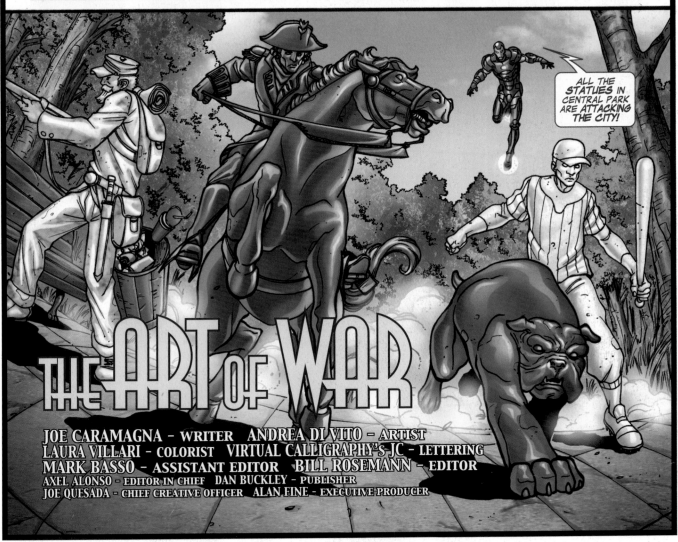

ALL THE STATUES IN CENTRAL PARK ARE ATTACKING THE CITY!

THE ART OF WAR

JOE CARAMAGNA - WRITER   ANDREA DI VITO - ARTIST
LAURA VILLARI - COLORIST   VIRTUAL CALLIGRAPHY'S JC - LETTERING
MARK BASSO - ASSISTANT EDITOR   BILL ROSEMANN - EDITOR
AXEL ALONSO - EDITOR IN CHIEF   DAN BUCKLEY - PUBLISHER
JOE QUESADA - CHIEF CREATIVE OFFICER   ALAN FINE - EXECUTIVE PRODUCER

KRAKOOM

CENTRAL PARK.

STICKS AND STONES CAN'T BREAK HULK'S BONES!

KLUDD

J.A.R.V.I.S., WHAT ARE WE DEALING WITH HERE?

MR. STARK, A BIO-SCAN OF YOUR ATTACKERS SHOWS NO LIVING TISSUE OR COGNITIVE ABILITY. THEY AREN'T ACTUALLY ALIVE.

THEY ARE BEING MANIPULATED REMOTELY. AND THE ENERGY SIGNATURE SURROUNDING THEM MATCHES THAT WHICH WE TYPICALLY FIND...

...IN ASGARD.

LOKI?

SEEMS SO.

CAN YOU TRACK ITS POINT OF ORIGIN?

TONY! WHERE ARE YOU GOING?!

SIR, THE ENERGY SOURCE IS MOVING NORTHEAST ON BROADWAY, TOWARDS CITY HALL, AT TWENTY-THREE AND A HALF MILES PER HOUR.

I'VE GOT A VISUAL--

13

THE NINE REALMS

Thor guides us through all the worlds of our dimension.

Nine Realms art: Haemi Jang

YGGDRAS
THE WORLD TRE

VANAHEIM
HOME OF THE VANIR,
WISE GODS OF OLD

MIDGARD
THE REALM OF
MORTALS

ASGARDIA
WHERE NOW
DWELL THE GODS
OF OLD ASGARD

NIFFLEHEIA
THE FROZEN UNDERWORL

SVARTALFHEIM
THE DARK FAERIE REALM

Vanaheim

Vanaheim is the realm of the Vanir, a race of wise and ancient beings; our Asgardian cousins. Once we warred against each other, but now we are staunch allies.

Midgard (Earth)

Home of the mortal humans who commonly refer to it as planet Earth. Thor was banished to Midgard to learn humility, and has defended it many times from numerous threats.

Svartalfheim

This dangerous land is home to the evil Dark Elves. They are ruled by their corrupt lord, Malekith, who once came close to conquering Asgard by using the Casket of Ancient Winters to unleash deadly snowstorms.

Niffleheim

Within this dark mist-shrouded underworld lies the foreboding ruler, Hela, Queen of the Dead. For eons she has tried to trap Thor in her kingdom, but she has always failed.

ASGARD ON ICE

JOE CARAMAGNA - WRITER   WELLINTON ALVES - PENCILER
ANDERSON SILVA - INKER   CARLOS LOPEZ - COLORIST   VC'S JC - LETTERING
MARK BASSO - ASSISTANT EDITOR   BILL ROSEMANN - EDITOR
AXEL ALONSO - EDITOR IN CHIEF   DAN BUCKLEY - PUBLISHER
JOE QUESADA - CHIEF CREATIVE OFFICER   ALAN FINE - EXECUTIVE PRODUCER

NOT WHAT YOU EXPECTED, FALCON?

I PICTURED MORE *LAND OF OZ* AND LESS... THE NORTH POLE.

KRAK

THE FROST GIANTS HAVE ATTACKED MY HOME AT ITS MOST *VULNERABLE*--WHILE THE ALL-FATHER TAKES REPOSE IN HIS *ODINSLEEP!*

WHAM

ODINSLEEP?

EVERY YEAR, THOR'S FATHER *HIBERNATES* TO RECHARGE HIS MOJO-- A LITERAL *POWER NAP.* HE COULD BE OUT FOR DAYS.

AND ASGARD'S *MAGICAL* DEFENSES ARE *DOWN* WHILE HE'S ASLEEP.

K-TANG

MAGIC. RIGHT.

YOU DOUBT THE MAGIC OF ASGARD, IRON MAN?

KRUNCH

THERE WAS A TIME WHEN PEOPLE THOUGHT **LIGHTNING** WAS MAGIC, TOO. THEN WE LEARNED ABOUT **IONIZATION** AND POSITIVE AND NEGATIVE CHARGES.

ALL "MAGIC" IS EXPLAINED BY SCIENCE. EVENTUALLY.

WHAT ABOUT **YOU**, CAP? DO YOU BELIEVE IN MAGIC?

I THINK IF A PERSON REALLY **BELIEVES** HE CAN DO SOMETHING--

--AND SETS HIS **MIND** TO IT--

--ANYTHING IS POSSIBLE.

WHAT I WOULDN'T GIVE TO RUN A FULL POLYSOMNOGRAPHIC STUDY ON ODIN WHILE HE'S SLEEPING...

FORGET IT, SAM. I DON'T BELIEVE IN MAGIC, BUT I **DO** BELIEVE HE'D KNOCK YOUR BLOCK OFF IF YOU WOKE HIM UP.

ISN'T ODIN'S PALACE THE **OTHER** WAY, THOR? WHAT IS THIS PLACE?

IF WE ARE TO DRIVE BACK OUR ATTACKERS AND RESTORE THIS KINGDOM TO ITS **GLORY**, WE MUST FREE THEIR MOST DANGEROUS **PRISONER**...

...MY BROTHER **LOKI!**

ARE-- ARE YOU SURE THIS IS A GOOD IDEA?

YOU KNOW HE HATES YOU, RIGHT?

LOKI IS THE ONE WHO SUMMONED ME WHEN ASGARD WAS ATTACKED. HE IS JUST AS INVESTED IN OUR FATHER'S KINGDOM AS I AM.

AND HE'S STILL MY BROTHER.

STAND BACK!

KER-FOOM

THUD

EVERY. SINGLE. TIME. SO PREDICTABLE!

MIDGARD?

EARTH. "ANTLERS" HERE THINKS HE'S GOING TO CONQUER THE EARTH.

THAT "BOX" IS ODIN ALL-FATHER'S "COLLECTION OF CURIOSITIES"—RELICS AND ARTIFACTS OF MYSTICAL PROPERTIES HE'S COLLECTED FOR THOUSANDS OF YEARS.

WITH THEIR LIMITLESS POWER IN MY GRASP, MIDGARD WILL NEVER KNOW WHAT HIT IT.

>RRRF!<

WHAT IS IT, YOU LOPSIDED POPSICLE?

RRAAGH!

YES. EVERYONE KNOWS THAT THOR IS THE ONLY ONE WORTHY TO LIFT MJOLNIR. DON'T YOU CREATURES READ?

THE DEAL WAS THOR FOR ODIN'S TREASURE. IT'S NOT MY FAULT YOU DON'T HAVE THE MENTAL CAPACITY TO--

RRRAARGH!

RRRAAAAARGH!

ACK!

THOOM

26

FOUL BEASTS...

KRAKKA-BA-DOOM!

...GO BACK FROM WHENCE YOU CAME!

HERE, LET ME GIVE YOU A LIFT.

TZARK

FLOOSH

THAT WAS AWESOME!

ARE YOU ALL RIGHT?

AS STRONG AS EVER. WHAT OF MY BROTHER?

HE TOOK HIS REWARD AND BAILED.

TRAITOROUS COWARD. SOMEDAY HE'LL GET WHAT IS COMING TO HIM.

SECRET BASES

Every hero and villain needs a place to unwind, to plan, or to plot, and today we are going to take a look at some of the coolest secret HQs in the Mighty Marvel Universe!

S.H.I.E.L.D. HELICARRIER

What makes the S.H.I.E.L.D. Helicarrier so cool is that there are several of them... so if one gets compromised there's always another ready to take its place.

HISTORY:

TONY STARK

Created by... you guessed it; Tony Stark, the Helicarrier is ideal for a swift response anywhere it is needed.

SECURITY AND ARMAMENTS:

Aircraft, highly trained agents, helicopters.

3	4	4
SECRECY FACTOR	POWER FACTOR	TECH FACTOR

AVENGERS TOWER

Okay, so Avengers Tower isn't particularly secret but it's still one of the greatest headquarters ever!

HISTORY:

Avengers Tower is the main tower of the Stark Tower Complex in Midtown Manhattan. Tony Stark donated the top three floors of this pad to the Avengers after their original HQ Avengers Mansion was destroyed.

SECURITY AND ARMAMENTS:

The Tower is protected by its very own residents: Earth's MightiestHeroes, the Avengers!

0	5	5
SECRECY FACTOR	POWER FACTOR	TECH FACTOR

33

CASTLE DRACULA

This place is by far the creepiest hideout ever. Nowhere else has chills and atmosphere like here!

HISTORY:

DRACULA

Built in the Carpathian Mountains of Transylvania, the castle has been invaded many times but always withstands any threats.

SECURITY AND ARMAMENTS:

Enter at your own peril – a vast army of the undead, black magic and hungry wolves await you!

4 SECRECY FACTOR **5** POWER FACTOR **1** TECH FACTOR

HYDRA SKY FORTRESS

HYDRA have got more secret hideouts than any other organisation but this sky base is easily the most impressive and the hardest to find!

SECURITY AND ARMAMENTS:

Heavily armed with deadly weaponry. If you want to take out a HYDRA HQ make sure you are fully prepared!

5 SECRECY FACTOR **3** POWER FACTOR **3** TECH FACTOR

CASTLE DOOM

Castle Doom might seem kind of old school as far as secret HQs go, but don't be fooled, Doctor Doom's lair comes with all mod-cons!

DOCTOR DOOM

HISTORY:

This 110-room castle overlooks Doomstadt, the capital of Doctor Doom's Kingdom of Latveria. It was built in the 16th century and is the centre of the Latverian government.

SECURITY AND ARMAMENTS:

Guarded by Doom-bots, Latverian guards, and force-fields.

1	5	4
SECRECY FACTOR	POWER FACTOR	TECH FACTOR

S.H.I.E.L.D. ALERT S.H.I.E.L.D. ALERT S.H.I.E.L.D. ALERT S.H.I.E.

S.H.I.E.L.D. NEEDS YOUR HELP. ONE OF OUR AGENTS HAS GONE MISSING IN ONE OF THESE SECRET HQS. LOOK AT THE CLUES FROM HIS RECENT REPORTS AND COMPARE THEM WITH THE DATA FILES TO SEE IF YOU CAN FIND THE AGENT'S LOCATION.

1. THE SECRET HEADQUARTERS APPEARS VERY OLD FASHIONED AT FIRST GLANCE.
2. NO. I AM NOT ON AN ISLAND. I REPEAT I AM NOT ON AN ISLAND.
3. I MISS MIDTOWN MANHATTAN. I WISH I WERE THERE NOW.
4. THERE ARE A LOT OF ARMED GUARDS OUTSIDE. THEY ARE PATROLLING THE GRAVEYARD.
5. I'M GLAD THIS HQ IS NOT IN THE AIR. I'M SCARED OF HEIGHTS.
6. THERE IS NOT A LIVING SOUL AROUND FOR MILES, EVEN LATVERIA IS LIVELIER THAN THIS PLACE.

THE MISSING S.H.I.E.L.D. AGENT WAS LAST SEEN AT:

HOW TO DRAW NICK FURY!

WHAT YOU NEED

Paper, a pencil, a rubber, coloured markers or coloured pencils.

STEP 1

Begin by roughly planning out Nick Fury's head, hands and cloak shape.

STEP 2

Sketch in the rough position of his limbs and body using oval shapes.

STEP 3

Now add in his pistol, mouth and eyepatch.

STEP 4

Draw in all the finer details including his pistol, face and clothing.

STEP 5

Erase your working lines and go over the final drawing with a fine black pen.

STEP 6

Finally, add some colour, using this picture as a guide!

5 THINGS YOU NEVER KNEW ABOUT...
CAPTAIN AMERICA

1. Cap was once banished to the faraway Dimension Z by Arnim Zola for over 10 years! It was there that he raised his son, Ian.

2. Steve Rogers is a very talented artist. He used to work as an illustrator to pay the bills!

3. Steve isn't the only one to have donned the iconic Captain America costume. Sam Wilson, the Falcon, has also donned his famous threads!

4. Long ago, Cap fought alongside Namor the Sub-Mariner and the original Human Torch, as a member of the Invaders, World War II's mightiest heroes!

5. Captain America was once deemed worthy enough to pick up Thor's mighty hammer! Fighting the sinister Serpent, he led the Avengers to victory with Mjolnir's power.

TAKING LIBERTIES

Captain America has been snapped by a photographer leaping into action! But... something has changed from the original. Can you find all seven changes?

ANSWER

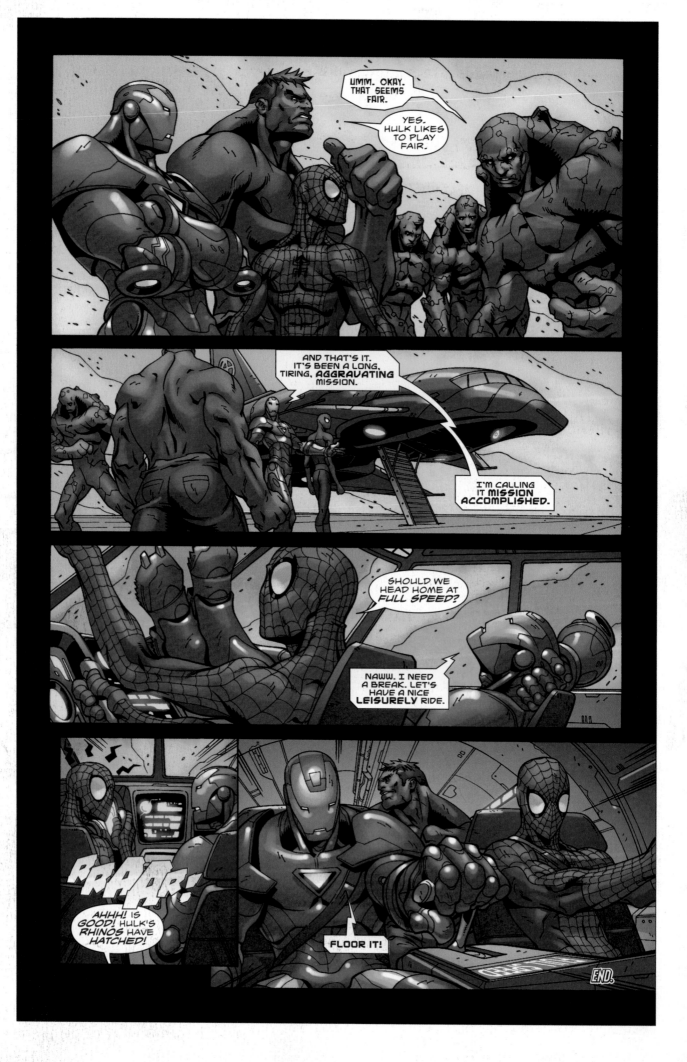

DARK AVENGERS

Iron Man's optical sensors are down! Use his thermo-scanners to work out which three of these heat signatures belong to the Avengers – and which belong to their greatest enemies!

A

B

C

DATA NOT FOUND

SCANNING...

CONNECTION ERROR!

D

UNKNOWN

E

F

ANSWERS - A-V, B-V, C-A, D-A, E-V, F-A.

Mark each box with either an 'A' for the Avengers or a 'V' for the villains.